Call Me Blessed

BECOMING
A MOTHER
OF HONOR

by Grace Ketterman

Beacon Hill Press of Kansas City
Kansas City, Missouri

Copyright 1997
by Beacon Hill Press of Kansas City

ISBN 083-411-6626

Printed in the
United States of America

Cover Design: Mike Walsh
Cover Photo: Westlight

Ketterman, Grace H.
    Call me blessed : becoming a mother of honor / Grace
    Ketterman.
        p.   cm.
    ISBN 0-8341-1662-6 (pbk.)
    1. Mothers.   2. Mother and child.   3. Motherhood—Reli-
gious aspects—Christianity.   4. Parenting.   I. Title.
HQ759.K477   1997
306.843'3—dc21   97-3835
                                                        CIP

10   9   8   7   6   5   4   3   2   1

INTRODUCTION

It's easy to formulate specific dreams for children. Most mothers would love to have a daughter who could someday be the homecoming queen. They would love a strong son who would be not only a sports hero but also a warm, tender protector of them.

Being able to brag about a child's successes in art, music, or academics is a great ego trip. Trouble is, it doesn't always happen that way.

Children are much more likely to have faulty physiques than grace and beauty. Sometimes, they are downright unattractive and awkward. Nothing they do seems to turn out right. They may have to work hard just to be average.

Although most mothers instinctively love their children, learning to properly nurture them is a process. Raising them in godliness is usually a matter of significant prayer and much trial and error. Take heart! God, the perfect Father, understands your desire to become a mother of honor. He has promised to equip you for the task at hand.

I've compiled this small book of dos and don'ts to help you on your journey. Most of the principles here are simple ones that have come from my years of experience as a child, physician, psychiatrist, mother, and grandmother. As you read, remember that above all the most important *do* is this: *Love and unconditionally accept your children despite their flaws.* Look for their inner beauty. Help them find their uniqueness, and bless them with your belief in their eventual usefulness in God's great plan.

You were created to become a mother of honor. Though the assignment lasts a lifetime, the rewards are eternal. The grace of God will enable you to be a mother whose children "rise up and call her blessed" (Prov. 31:28).

—*Grace Ketterman, M.D.*

DO PLAY WITH YOUR CHILD

One of my most delightful memories is of my family playing games together. There were seven children and two parents—nine in all—around the dining table. In the center was a dishpan full of freshly popped corn and a bowl of apples. In an old-fashioned matchbox were little squares of cardboard with names of all the books of the Bible, four copies of them. The goal was to see who could get the most sets of four names of each book by trading cards. We called it Bible Authors.

Playing with your children creates a unique bond that lasts a lifetime—and beyond. When a child has laughed with you in loving play, he or she will find it much easier to respect your boundaries and to accept your shortcomings.

Play comes in many forms. It starts in infancy with tickling, cooing, and gentle tossing. It progresses to rolling a ball or toy car, building with blocks, and on to pretending tea parties or toy soldier battles. It includes walks, swinging, and teeter-tottering. Later, it involves board games like Candyland or Monopoly. Whatever is the most fun for you is likely to be fun for your child too.

In all your play, be careful to balance winning with losing. Throughout life, one will suffer losses; learning to lose and promptly resuming play again can teach children how to cope with failure without giving up. Don't let winning become an occasion for gloating and arrogance. Help your child be a fair winner, as well as a brave loser.

Above all, remember: "A merry heart doeth good like a medicine" (Prov. 17:22, KJV). Keep an attitude of playfulness if you want a truly happy family!

DON'T BE PICKY

"Sally, sit still; you've been wriggling in your chair all during dinner."

"Sally, quit twisting your hair! It's going to get knots in it."

"If you don't stop sniffing, Sally, I'm going to scream! You know how that irritates me!"

"Your room is a pigsty, Sally; I can't stand it another day!"

No doubt every mom has yelled one or more of these jibes at a child with an annoying habit. But when Sally hears too many, too often, her attitudes (and yours) will show it. Sally will either learn to avoid you, or she will become so anxious the habits will worsen.

To avoid being excessively critical, try the following ideas:

1. Select the worst (most irritating) habit. Talk kindly to your child, explaining how the habit bothers others. Interpret that behavior as coming about because the child is worried, upset, or bored.

2. Get your child's cooperation in formulating a plan for breaking the habit. A "worry stone," a tiny rock a boy can rub in his pocket, can calm a fidgety lad. A new comb may help Sally learn to comb her hair instead of twisting it.

3. Compliment your child's improvement, and only gently remind him or her of forgetting. A reward of some playtime with you on the weekend can be a great motivator for breaking annoying habits.

4. Take a careful look at yourself. Are you expecting too much? Maybe you sound more angry than you realized. Ease back a bit, take some time, correct with love, and you will accomplish your task more efficiently.

DO BE AN EFFECTIVE TEACHER

A mother can be a child's best teacher about life. It's tempting to want your child to become an academic genius, but intelligence and success are no substitute for basic life skills.

Mom, think about the sort of person you'd like your child to be in adult years. Would you like your son to show the gentle spirit of a truly strong man? Then model such a spirit, and teach him how to practice it. Perhaps you'd like your daughter to evidence the quiet confidence that can be her strength. Then be both tactfully corrective of her errors and affirming of her good efforts. Teaching these and all values happens in the ordinary moments of our daily lives.

Your example is the best teaching tool you have, mothers! As you model an open, teachable attitude and a gentle, confident manner, you will create the best climate possible for growth in your children.

Few people today have a normal sense of spirituality. You can instill this priceless gift into the hearts of your children by your example. Be careful not to use God to scare and punish your kids, but use His Word to establish guidelines for life. Follow His example of grace. After any correction or consequence, kindly be certain your children have learned the most lessons possible. Then forgive them, reinstate them in your unconditional love, and never bring up what is finished.

Not only can you teach your children about

life in the present, but also, with God's help, you will teach them about eternal life in the Father!

DO BE TRANSPARENT

It has worked well for me to practice the art of being open, honest, and vulnerable with people. This has especially been true as a mother. I cherished the many stories my mother and grandmother told me about their growing-up years. I could identify with their work, their play, and especially with their mistakes.

All of us need to have a few secrets we may choose to never share with anyone. But having too many secrets indicates an excess of shame and a fear of inadequacy. They tend to breed into a family a sense of fear that is uncomfortable and confusing.

Being transparent means that you know yourself—how you feel, what you think, and how to honestly and appropriately express yourself. I have known moms who honestly feel angry with a child's misbehavior. They believe, however, it's wrong to be angry, so they try to act grieved. Children, who accurately sense our feelings, are confused. Is Mom really sad? Or is she mad? Sadness creates guilt in a child, but Mom's anger is more likely to result in rebellion—pitting anger against anger.

If you really are angry, express that emotion in

these three ways: (1) Put your feeling into a clear word: "I am very irritated!" (2) State clearly why you feel irritated: "I've called you to dinner three times, and you haven't come"; and (3) State firmly what you will do: "I will eat with the rest of the family after calling you only once. Next time, you may eat cold leftovers alone." The feelings are understood, the choice is clear, the anger is over!

These simple steps apply also to fear, sorrow, joy, or excitement. Learn to share both your life experiences and your feelings with your children. Teach them how to recognize and express their own emotions so they can live a transparent life.

DON'T FOCUS ON NEGATIVES

What is your usual response to your children's requests? Requests they are full of, from wanting a cookie to needing the car. Some mothers, I've noticed, routinely say, "I should say not!" "No, you can't use the phone! I'm waiting for a call."

A child's response to constant negatives will vary from a distressed despondency to angry rebellion. How you mothers answer your children's multiple wants will determine the outcome.

I've never recommended that mothers be permissive. But neither can I recommend that your impulsive answer usually be "No!" In fact, it's wise to think first about whether a "Yes" reply would be harmful. Next, ask yourself if it might even be a good thing. By considering both pros and cons, you will be able to give wise reasons for your replies. It's most important that once you decide, you stick with the course whether your child likes it or not. You can even help your child reach the decision with you by sharing your thought process.

Not only do you benefit your family by offering positive answers whenever possible, but also reacting lovingly to your child's mistakes makes correction bearable. Don't forget, love often can be tough. Jim, a young friend of mine, makes lots of mistakes. When his mom corrects him, she states clearly and emphatically what he did wrong. She helps him see what made it wrong and what he can do next time to prevent the error. Then they hug each other, and the day moves on with hope and love.

Finally, your positive attitude will create sunshine in the midst of a storm. It's rainy, and that means fretful kids and mud tracks in the hallway. So go to plan B. Create coziness with hot chocolate or fruit drinks and a special treat. Bad weather invites reading or telling stories. Coloring or creative play with blocks can make you all enjoy rainy days. But it's your attitude, Mom, that gets it going.

You'll feel better, too, Mother, when you master the affirming, positive attitude!

DO LOVE YOUR CHILD'S FATHER

A wife loving her husband should be a given in any marriage. Unfortunately, that's simply not true! Husbands often are absorbed in their own projects, whether it's TV, sports, or repainting the house. Legitimate and even wonderful as these activities may be, they can consume too much time and energy, leaving all too little for you or the kids. Sometimes, husbands are gruff and grouchy, so they are even harder to love!

Children, however, are genetically part of each parent, and they have a unique sort of attachment to their dad—even when he doesn't measure up to who he ought to be. And children know how their parents feel about each other. They even know when a parent develops an affair with someone else. So your job, moms, is to deal with your inner feelings and attitudes. Make those loving and understanding.

The Bible says, "As he thinketh in his heart, so is he" (Prov. 23:7a, KJV). I once heard a psychiatrist say in a seminar, "If you keep your thoughts straight and decisions wise, your feelings and attitudes will also be right."

When you find yourself frustrated and upset with your husband, don't give in to those feelings. Instead, stop and think:

1. What makes him behave as he does?

2. Does he realize how much he neglects us?
3. Without nagging, can I help him see that we love him and need more of him?
4. Have I shown him unconditional love?
5. Have I required the children to tell him directly how they feel and what they need of him?
6. Is there a counselor who can help us both become loving again?

Love is not just a feeling. It is a decision, a discipline, and a commitment. Love must be tender and tough. There are certain abusive situations that demand a love so tough that we say, "Enough!" Unless that is your situation, consistently show your husband respect, affection, and sincerity. Your children will learn to respect both you and him if you do so. You have the opportunity to create the most positive environment possible for all of you to thrive!

DO LOOK PRETTY

It's very easy to slip into habits of carelessness at home. When you have to go to work, you must put considerable energy into dressing just right, fixing your hair stylishly, and putting on your makeup. It's all too easy, however, to let your appearance become unbecoming at home.

Many moms with small children are so busy

refereeing their fights, feeding them, keeping their toys in order, and washing their clothes that they slip into the habit of neglecting themselves. They may even fail to watch their weight and maintain good hygiene.

Children notice many things, and they are sensitive to their mother's appearance. By school age, they compare you to their teacher or to the mothers of friends. They want most of all to see a smile and to feel the look of love and humor on your face. They like the glossy, soft appearance of freshly shampooed hair. They delight in the scent of light perfume. They will notice your clothing too. Even my 18-month-old grandson grins at the playful kitten painted on my sweatshirt.

Your child deserves to believe that you are the prettiest mom among all the second grade mothers. And you will be if you love and have fun with him or her and take good care of yourself.

Here are some things mothers can do to be beautiful:

1. Walk so closely with God that His love lights your home through you.
2. Take bits of time for yourself—to read a little, listen to music, just think and pray. Requiring your children to take naps or have a quiet time can provide a few minutes dur-

ing the day. After bedtime, in the evening, take some more time for yourself.

3. Look for bargains in clothing, and plan your wardrobe to be interchangeable. A few garments worn with different items will look like a new outfit.

4. Show self-respect without arrogance. When you are confident, you will inevitably be a wiser, better mom.

A fringe benefit of looking lovely for your children and yourself is likely to be the admiration of your husband. So make a commitment to yourself to look pretty and feel pretty too.

DON'T LECTURE

When I was little, I did many wrong things. For example, I pouted when I had to entertain my little sister. At times, I was downright mean to her. I didn't do all my work up to my mother's expectations. I needed correcting for sure! But I didn't appreciate Mom's lectures.

Those attempts at teaching me would start with a normal tone of voice, but they were long lectures. As they went on, Mom's voice would rise. Before long, she seemed to me to be screaming. Often she would weep in the intensity of her effort to make me sorry. I was indeed sorry, because I wanted her approval. But I became more and more resentful of her excessive methods. I can still identify profound sadness, anger, guilt, and even fear that I could be the death of my own mother. These feelings, along with the feeling of utter hopelessness of ever pleasing Mom, left me with memories of many sad times in my childhood.

During countless sessions of therapy with families, I have seen a parent launch into a lecture similar to my mother's. Invariably, I've observed the child addressed roll her eyes or slump his shoulders, trying to tune out the sound. Lectures to correct kids simply don't work. They create resistance instead.

So how about trying something that will work? Here are steps I have used with good success.

Give some time out to your child and take some yourself. Think carefully about what was wrong and why the child did it. Collect all the puzzle pieces, and try to see the entire picture clearly. When you both are somewhat calm, discuss the event in a problem-solving way. Help your child discover as many facts as he or she can. When you hear evidence that the needed lesson is understood, the correction is accomplished.

All that's left, then, is the forgiving, a tender hug, and assurance that this is in the past. If you follow these patterns, adapted to your own personality, your children will work hard to avoid wrongs.

And years later you will rejoice in Prov. 31:28*a:* "Her children [shall] rise up and call her blessed."

DO LOOK AT YOUR CHILD

Some years ago my youngest daughter had her first child. As I spent time with them, I observed her doing instinctively a very important thing. As long as she could when he was awake, she gently swayed him in her lap and focused intently on his eyes. He, in turn, followed her eyes as if life depended on it!

Later I read a research article that showed the value of such eye contact. It seems that mother-child bonding greatly depends on such mutual gazing.

You see, at birth babies can see only shades of black and white. It's weeks later that they begin to detect color and define the facial outlines of their caretaker. Everyone has slightly different eye color, but all people have a black center of their eyes called the "pupil." And they all have the white, shiny part of their eye called the "sclera." So when a mother cares for her tiny baby, all the baby can clearly see is her eyes. When the Bible says, "I will guide thee with mine eye," I suspect that's because

God knew He'd put that bonding instinct into mothers and babies (Ps. 32:8, KJV).

If you glance frequently at your child with eyes full of love, you will be creating a sense of trust. That tiny grandson is now a schoolboy. I watch his unabashed ability to look directly, confidently into the eyes of people he is with. I believe that was learned in his mother's lap as an infant.

Perhaps you were too busy or didn't know your baby needed such eye contact. Don't worry. Start now. Create a game to see who can communicate the most love by just looking into each other's eyes. Practice looking lovingly into your child's eyes whenever you speak. Remind him or her to look at you when you talk together.

Good eye contact requires a preponderance of positive emotions. Learn to identify how you feel. If you are disgusted, angry, or irritated, wait until you change such threatening emotions to tough love. Then look at your child with a no-nonsense but caring expression. Practice in front of a mirror.

As you learn to express love—tender *or* tough —to your child, give plenty to yourself. Christ instructed us to love our neighbor *as* ourselves. That's especially true with you and your child. If you regard yourself as a person of worth, it will come through as love to your child.

DO BE A CHILD COMFORTER

When Lester was only five, he often awoke at night terrified. A bad dream or a storm could startle him awake with a sense of panic. He recalls running to his parents' bed, needing to cuddle into his mother's arms for safety. But not once can he recall being allowed that privilege. Instead, he was sent, lonely and scared, back to his own bed. Had his mother even gone with him and lovingly tucked him under the covers, he would have experienced comfort.

Be sure that you do not repeat that mom's mistake. Comforting a hurt or scared child will not make a scaredy-cat or baby out of him. Instead, it will strengthen those fragile bonds of trust and bind you together in love.

How does a mom best comfort a child? The answer depends on two things—that child's age and temperament. Until the age of 10, most kids need physical closeness. A long, tender hug or being held on Mom's lap restores security. Older children often are embarrassed by being treated "like a baby," so they may be helped best by your presence nearby and your words of reassurance.

One of the mistakes many supernurturing mothers make is to overreact to a troubled child. Many such mothers have endured various and painful life events. When a child of theirs suffers similar trauma, they not only feel the child's distress but also vividly recall their own hurts. In overcomforting their children, they unconsciously seek healing for their own memories.

Serious overreaction to a hurt child can teach a dramatic degree of self-pity. Kids may even learn to look for slights or react to mosquito bites as if they were dog bites! It is often such superreactions by mothers that worry dads.

So be careful to balance your tender love and comfort with reality. Encourage a hurting child to be brave and reassure him or her of eventual healing. A colorful Band-Aid can become a badge of honor.

Later, when the pain is in the heart rather than on the surface like a skinned knee, comfort is more difficult. It takes more listening than talking. Questions to help the victim talk about the rejection, loss, or disappointment allows more healing than well-intended "You poor thing!" comments. As a hurt youngster pours out the words describing the painful event, he or she can be guided to solutions. This technique helps kids recognize their own strengths and empowers them to use them, not just at the time of the trauma but for all their lives.

Your skill in comforting can help build a healthy child. If in that process you, too, are healed, that's an additional blessing.

DON'T BE PERMISSIVE

Why, I wondered, would such a gorgeous teenager be in the office of a "shrink," as all my young patients called me. Tricia was neatly dressed in a plaid skirt with a bright top in her high school colors. Her blond hair looked like silk, and her green eyes like fine china. Yet when I focused on the whole of her, I saw the drooping shoulders, downcast face, and the veil of her blond hair hiding her features. Her appearance corroborated her words: "Dr. Grace, I'm just *so* depressed. And I've been depressed for three years."

Further talk revealed some significant facts. Her family from a distant state had moved many times to keep up with the growing degree of financial success. Because the family could afford it, they had most of the household work done by servants. Tricia had no responsibilities at home. Her grades ranged from a rare C to several Fs. She was allowed to go where she wished, with whomever she pleased, to stay as long as she wanted. Tricia had no boundaries. So she used drugs in an effort to be happy, and for a few hours at a time they seemed to work.

While the story is extreme, it is true. In lesser degrees, it is true of many young people these days. Surely all parents want their kids to be happy. Rightly so! What it seems they do not know is this—happiness comes from being productive. Children are happy who help around the house, earn Mom's praise, and feel her gratitude. When they study and earn decent grades, they can feel proud and experience success. When they have clear boundaries, they will not be likely to waste their energy in manipulating you to find out if they can do unacceptable things.

Boundaries must be flexible but consistent. They must gradually expand as your child matures. But maintaining them is crucially important.

Every mom sets her own boundaries, and they often cause frustration. But without them you'd never be able to do your job. So avoid being permissive; keep the limits well defined and consistently enforced. It'll be good for both you and your child.

DO KNOW THE EMOTIONAL NEEDS OF YOUR CHILD

Having my newborn baby placed in my arms was a shocking experience. She was so tiny, so totally helpless, and so dependent on me. There would be no end to the relationship with this new life. How could I possibly meet her needs from now on?

I must confess I stumbled many times, making countless mistakes. Most of those were transient errors and left few scars. A few were more severe, and I had to apologize when she grew up. Graciously, she's forgiven me.

But much of my panic could have been prevented had I known that day in the hospital that my baby's needs are really few and fairly simple. That is not to say they are *easy* to supply, but at least it is possible to meet them.

The first need is for physical care and safety. Children need food, warmth, cuddling, rocking, and playing with. They need exercise and freedom to explore and learn within safe boundaries. They need medical care, immunizations against deadly diseases, and regular checkups. These areas of care are well known to most moms.

The emotional needs are more challenging. Consider the following needs, and see if you identify with them:

1. *The need of unconditional love.* You've read about that in the Introduction. You must find a way to accept each child exactly as he or she looks or learns to behave, no matter what. Do remember how God loves you—even at your worst.

2. *The need of approval.* Every child needs to know you are proud of him or her. Early on, that pride is easy—it comes naturally with the firsts: first smile, first tooth, first step,

first word. Only a bit later, the first two-year-old rebellion challenges Mom's confidence. You must see each stage as planned by God to help your child become a successful adult.

3. *The need of predictability.* In similar situations, your child needs to know the response that can be counted on from you. If one day you shout when the milk is spilled, but the next day you ignore it, he or she has to spill it on the third day to see what you'll do next. Try to be consistent, and your child will learn to adapt.

4. *The need of laughter.* Life becomes heavy much of the time. It's so important that you keep the gift of a merry heart active in your family.

I trust that as you practice meeting these few but so vital needs of your children, the surplus will fill your own heart. God loves you as you are. He will correct you so He can be well pleased with you. He is faithful and totally predictable. His is the original merry heart. May your needs be fully met by Him!

DO BE A MOTHER WHO PRAYS

I will not fully understand prayer in this life. Neither do I fully comprehend nuclear physics. But I am certain both are facts of life and that each works just as God the Creator designed them to.

My childhood was spent during the unbearable years of the Great Depression. Throughout the world people suffered, struggling to exist without the barest essentials of life.

During those years, there were always 10 people at our dinner table. Often, various additional relatives came to stay for periods of time. Thanks to hard work and a good farm we always had enough food, which we shared with many who did not.

Whenever we had to buy new shoes or other wearing apparel, my mother prayed. She asked God to provide well-fitting, durable items. He did! Many times I wore shoes that my older sister had used until she outgrew them.

Plagues of grasshoppers and chinch bugs could strip a field of grain in minutes. Mother prayed, as our entire family joined in, every morning that God would protect us and our crops. He did! We sometimes lost parts of a field, but never did we lose all of our varied fields of grain.

Mother's ministry of prayer was backed up by hard work and strict economy. Even a bent pin was not discarded but gently straightened and used. My mother never wrote a check, but she had never-failing access to God's heavenly bank account.

Her ministry became my example. I'm trying

very hard to pass on that example to my children. They know that prayer works—though, like me, they can't explain how.

In 2 Tim. 1:5, Paul wrote, "I am reminded of your sincere faith, a faith that dwelt first in your grandmother Lois and your mother Eunice and now, I am sure, dwells in you." Your prayers and your faith are a priceless legacy for your children.

DON'T BE RIGID

"Please, Mom! All the kids are going out for pizza after the game, and I wanna go too. I know it'll keep me out half an hour after my curfew. But I'm almost always home on time. I study hard, and I think I've earned just this once to stay later!" Rod's plea was really convincing. He told the truth.

Mom was strongly tempted to give in. He was a good boy, almost 16. But she recalled his older sister. Giving in to her too often had ruined her. In her search for excessive freedom, she had left home without ever going to college or making anything good out of her life. Mom decided to stay firm. Rod would have to be home at his usual time, and she would go and bring him home.

Rod was home on time; Mom held to her rules. But the price was high! Rod began to sneak out, reduced his studying, and became sullen. Finding out that rigidity could be as destructive as permissiveness was a big lesson for Mom.

Behaviors like testing the limits and rebelling against rigidity can look identical. Mom, you must take stock now and then. It is necessary to know your child's temperament and to review living habits. If, like Rod, your young person is basically responsible and follows most rules willingly, he or she will benefit from some flexibility. If, however, your offspring is like Rod's sister, always pushing the boundaries and evidencing too little success and responsibility, that one needs firmer boundaries.

Some kids are too close to the edge to be clear about. Ask a friend or teacher. A youth counselor in church can offer an objective perspective.

Consider the extremes, and you will find the positive middle of the road. Meantime, be honest with your children—tell them you're not always sure what's best, and share your concerns with them. Avoid a harsh, controlling attitude, and stay loving. As long as love controls, many mistakes will be forgiven.

Being flexible will offer great benefits for both you, Mom, and your child.

DO LOVE YOUR CHILDREN'S FRIENDS

Sally's mother strictly forbade her to associate with three of her schoolmates. She knew they would get into trouble when they were together. Sally was a bright, independent teenager, and she couldn't just give in to Mom's demands. So she spent every possible moment with them in school. She sneaked notes to them in class and waited for stolen moments when she could talk with them by phone. She defended their faults and soon began to copy their misbehaviors.

Carol's mother, on the other hand, learned to welcome her child's friends into their home. She managed to supply games and snacks, making them feel welcome—at home. She nurtured their souls with God's love as she fed their bodies with her cookies. She waited and prayed for her child to discern the problem friends' weak spots. Instead of condemning them, she prayed for them sometimes with her child. Mom seemed to walk a narrow line, taking the risks she did. But Carol never strayed far from her family's values and grew up to be a well-adjusted, happy woman.

Accept your children's friends, realizing there is always an exception. Rarely, you may have to exclude a friend of your child's—one who is too damaged to help. If you must, do so gently and with compassion and prayer.

I again remind you of God's promise that Jesus, His Son, "is made unto us wisdom, and righteousness, and sanctification, and redemption" (1 Cor. 1:30, KJV).

DON'T LET ANGER CONTROL YOU

For years our culture has advocated the bumper sticker philosophies—"Let it all hang out!" and "If it feels good, do it!" And people everywhere have done just that. They have hit and yelled out their rage. They've ignored the pain that their uncontrolled tongues have dumped on others. It's well past time to learn how to handle anger and its explosive damage.

Mother, you have an opportunity to instill the ability to express anger in a useful way. First, let me remind you that the apostle Paul admonished the Ephesians, "Be angry but do not sin; do not let the sun go down on your anger" (4:26). Many times the Bible mentions the wrath of God. Anger is not sin, but the way it's expressed certainly can be.

Because anger is so powerful, it can block out our rational thinking. So these three rules work in controlling rage by restoring our reasoning:

1. Name the feeling you have. You may be a

bit irritated, very angry, or outright furious. Thinking of the best-fitting word, you see, triggers your mind to take control over your emotions. Teach this step to your children. When they have the words to say, they are not so likely to act out their anger.

2. Explain why you feel as you do. Probably you are frustrated because you've reminded a child repeatedly to do a task. And she has still forgotten it. This step further engages your thoughts, so your anger is no longer out of control.

3. Decide what *you* will do about step two. Most of us find ourselves telling the other person where they can take this problem and what they can do with it. Usually that's not effective. What does work is a definite statement. "I will remind you only once about your homework. If you fail to do it, you will take the consequences of staying after school for study hall." Not only does this focus your anger on an answer, but also it makes clear to your child whose problem and job it really is.

As you practice these three steps to anger control, you can see how much happier you and your family will be.

DO BE A LISTENER

"But Mary kept all these things, pondering them in her heart" (Luke 2:19). One of the qualities of Mary that I admire the most was her ability to be silent and to think deeply. Many people do not recognize this ability, and many others practice it poorly. Are you a good listener?

One mother I came to know well was a terrible listener. She argued, lectured, even yelled. Her family avoided her whenever possible. At last she did learn to listen. But here's why, as she later told me. She discovered that by listening carefully, she could plan her arguments even more successfully!

The purpose of listening is to gain understanding and to practice obedience. A Jewish rabbi, a dear friend, told me that theirs is a listening religion. Nearly eight columns of fine print in the *Cruden's Concordance* list scriptures about hearing. Sometimes Christians become more involved with lectures and debates. Mothers need to be good teachers, but we do that best through our examples, godly wisdom, and brief, concise sentences.

Listening must be done with the heart as well as the ears to be effective. Usually, children will talk if mothers listen in this manner. Sometimes you may need to ask questions. Be certain your questions are a genuine search for facts, not a means of cornering and condemning your child. Watch your progeny's face to observe the inner feelings about an issue. Look at the posture and hands. Are they rigid and tense? Or drooping and hopeless? As you read body language and listen to your child's feelings with your heart, you will be able to communicate understanding. You and your child can thus learn to negotiate and solve problems. You will find you are friends!

I hope you have experienced the silent, loving listening God the Father does for you. Read all you can about Mary, the mother of Jesus. I trust her example will teach you, too, to be quiet, to listen thoughtfully, and to hear with the heart of your child!

DON'T BE YOUR CHILD'S PEER

It's very important to be your child's friend as well as parent. And balancing these two roles can be a complicated juggling act. From disciplining youngsters to coping with teenagers, this challenge exists. It continues on, even when you become a grandmother!

"Mom, I hate you!" yelled eight-year-old Kent. She had just reminded him for the umpteenth time to pick up his Legos and come to dinner. She was angry, and her voice had become harsh.

"Kent, don't you talk to me like that!" she responded to his outburst. Without realizing it, the two of them interacted like peers engaged in verbal combat. Dinner was more a time for a stomachache than for nourishment. Life for Kent and Mom was a drag!

Kim at 14 was becoming a beautiful, vivacious teen. She had many friends, and they were welcome in her home. But she was becoming uneasy about the way her mother acted around her friends. She dressed in teen styles. More and more, she developed a teen vocabulary. She even flirted some with the guys.

When Kim finally explained her discomfort to her mom, she replied, "But, Kim, I'm only trying to make your friends feel at home. I think they like me this way!" At last, Kim gave up trying to help Mom understand. She began to spend more time away from home.

Mothers need to keep two concepts clear. One is their position or status. Mom may not always be right, but she is always Mom! The other is her attitude. As long as she is secure in her position, Mom can be playful, tender, firm, or downright stern. But she cannot succeed if she descends to child-to-child combat as did Kent's mother. Nor can she keep a healthy relationship with her teen if she chooses to compete as Kim's mother did.

Be sure to keep your own interests in life active and yet reserve enough energy to be involved with your kids. Balance tender, tough, and protective love. Gradually relinquish your children. Be a friend with your child as much as you can while maintaining that foundation of solid mothering.

DO FOCUS YOUR CHILD ON GOALS

One of the best treasures my mother left to me in her legacy was the conviction that I had a reason for living. As far back as I can recall, I believed that I was born of love by God's design, not by an accident of passion. I was taught that every task I did should glorify God (*and* please my mother!). He had a job for me to do. Big or insignificant, it was my responsibility to discover that job and do it the very best I could. Not a bad belief!

In their well-intentioned rearing of children, many mothers forget to guide their offspring toward establishing goals and working to reach them. They only ask that their children be happy and that they make good grades. Without realizing it, moms sometimes sell their kids short and expect far too little of them.

Long ago, I memorized this bit of incredible wisdom. "The end of life is *not* to be happy. The purpose of life is to have it matter, to make some difference that you have lived at all. Happiness in the ancient, noble sense is given to those who use to their best ability whatever talents God has given them. It is reserved for those who stretch to the farthest possible extent all of the resources of the mind and heart!"

Please teach your children that each of them can make a difference in his or her own special compartment of the world. God does have a plan for them—and you. Together, keep looking for their unique talents, their special gifts from God. Help each one to value those gifts, develop them, and eventually use them to make a better world. What a difference a wise mother's teaching can make.

DON'T OVERREACT

Dorian at 16 was a "hunk," as the teenage girls would say. He was good at sports, could have been an outstanding scholar, and was at once a joy and frustration to his teachers and parents. He had been increasingly rebellious in his search for independence.

Mother waited up night after night for her son, often worried because he was late returning from a game or a date. She suspected he'd been engaging in sex with his current girlfriend. She worried about drug abuse and drinking. Last Friday he'd smelled of alcohol when she kissed him good night. But this evening was a nightmare. He was downright drunk, sick to his stomach, and bleary-eyed. Surely this couldn't be happening to Dorian!

And, of course, it didn't *happen* to him. He'd been making bad decisions that were likely to damage him in serious ways. Mom wanted to spank him and hug him—to pull him back to the protection she gave him as a little boy. But she couldn't. After much thought and prayer, here's what she did do.

She found a time when Dorian was in a reasonable frame of mind. Over a soda they talked in a small restaurant for a long time. Mom defined her problems and got him to think about his perspective. She was able to make clear the possible options he had and just what the consequences could be for each one. She challenged him to make a choice and privately prayed it would be a wise one. Eventually, she and Dorian's father sought brief counseling to help them all work successfully to redeem Dorian's future.

I've seen other parents rage at a rebellious child, give threats, or endlessly ground the young person, prompting even further rebellion.

Through prayer and responding to God's wisdom, you, too, can avoid overreacting. You can be, with God's power, a redemptive influence in your child's life.

DO BUILD YOUR CHILD'S SELF-ESTEEM

Self-esteem is not a quality of arrogance or egoism. It is, instead, the grateful awareness that I am important to God—not because I'm so terrific but because of who I am in Him. If, as He said, humankind was created in His very image, we must be very special! He can, indeed, make us so.

But God has delegated to mothers the challenge to build that confident, self-respecting quality in children that we call self-esteem. It may more accurately be called God's child's esteem!

There are some clearly defined ways you can help your child develop an inner core of strength. The first is the certainty of unconditional acceptance. If your child *knows* you love him or her no matter what, there will be hope for recovery from errors.

Next, your child must learn to live free from guilt—most of the time. Teach each one to acknowledge wrongs, to repent of them, to make restitution, and to avoid repeating the wrong. Avoid laying expectations on your child that are impossible to achieve. Teach the principle of doing one's best, and let your offspring know your pride in both efforts and successes. When there is failure, give help in learning from the experience and renewing his or her efforts.

Self-esteem builds on successes. And though children do need to learn to accept loss and failure, get up, and move on, they must also savor the taste of enough successes to keep them motivated. In both work and play, help your children set realistic goals, then cheer them on until they reach them. Enjoy with them the thrill of success. Many times this grand thought enters my awareness, which I like to think is from God. "God, aren't You and I a great team? With all Your resources, You help me to help others. But You actually *need* even me to be Your arms, voice, and love." Without Him, we are not much. But He desires us to be the expression of himself to others. What a way to live!

DON'T HIT

Today there rages a huge controversy—to spank or not to spank a misbehaving child. I once adhered to the "wooden spoon" philosophy. It was believed that such a small piece of equipment could not hurt a child. But I began to hear from parents who used one that even a wooden spoon could raise welts and leave bruises. With the immense stress of today's world, even careful parents can overpunish.

Now, I will say that a rare, carefully and cere-moniously delivered set of swats may not seriously abuse a child. My mother spanked me twice. She took me firmly by the hand through the kitchen and dining room into the parlor. There she bent me over her lap and with her hand swatted my well-padded seat. Years later she explained a useful principle. She walked through the house to give herself time to gain control of her anger. I'm not certain she knew it also gave me time to realize my wrongdoing and to become properly repentant.

Any physical punishment should be rare if it is to have significance. It must be preceded by a clear definition of the misdeed. And it must be followed by forgiveness and restoration to love.

Other consequences that successfully replace spanking are firm restraint, a serious look, and a stern voice. The use of time-out can be highly effec-tive. Always use the principles of clearly defining the wrong, stating the right action, expecting better behavior, and finally forgiving and loving to com-plete the ceremony.

"He who spares the rod hates his son," says Prov. 13:24. But I believe the rod is that of the shep-herd: "Thy rod and thy staff, they comfort me," says Ps. 23:4. The shepherd's rod is always in the watchful grasp of the caretaker—to guide the lambs from straying and protect them from danger.

Mom, provide that priceless, protective rod of your presence and guidance—in the tradition of Jesus, our Good Shepherd.

DO PROTECT YOUR CHILDREN

When I was only five, immunization against diphtheria was new. I recall my parents' excitement over the possibility that no one would ever again have to die from that often fatal disease. Mother insisted that I be included with my school-age siblings in receiving the lifesaving injection. Our wonderful country doctor told me I was the bravest person of all because I didn't cry when he poked the needle in my small arm.

Few moms today realize the anxieties of parents in years past over killer epidemics of various fatal diseases. Yet mothers today do protect their children with every visit to their pediatrician or family doctor. The care kids routinely receive is all too often taken for granted.

What many mothers forget, however, is the protection their children need from other ills. The risks of peer pressure, materialism, and spiritual doubts have become paramount as concerns we face for our children.

Once peer pressure has captured a teenager, it is very difficult to extricate him or her. It's far easier to prevent such problems. Here are the actions you can take to protect your child from both social and spiritual ills:

1. Build a strong friendship with your child as well as maintaining good mothering.
2. Teach your child to recognize peer pressure and the inner insecurity that makes him or her vulnerable to it.
3. Constantly help build genuine self-esteem in your child to avoid most of that insecurity.
4. Live and breathe the truth of your child's acceptance in Jesus Christ. As both you and he or she seek to live lives that please Him, peer pressure will be significantly lessened.
5. Maintain a safety net of private prayer to undergird your child.
6. Be watchful for signs of straying away from the right path, and use every possible resource to get your child back in line.

There is no insurance policy against waywardness or rebellion by children. But if you trained them up in the way they should go, you can trust God to bring them back safely.

DO BE AN EFFECTIVE WORKING MOTHER

If you don't absolutely have to work outside your

home, especially with preschoolers, don't! But I'm practical enough to know many of you have no choice. Perhaps you need some outside productivity to keep your sanity. Obviously, many families need both incomes to survive, and certainly single moms have to work.

Whatever your reason, here are some ideas to help you and your family live happily, even though you're gone all day.

1. Avoid feeling guilty because you work. Guilty moms tend to pamper their kids to make up for their absence, thereby spoiling them. Explain to your family why you are working and that you need their help.

2. Set up a regular family meeting to discuss all issues—job assignments, schoolwork, scheduled activities, budget items, your needs as well as theirs.

3. Keep your priorities in the right order. Though I've always worked, my children knew I adored them because I did! And I showed it by taking time off to be a den mother, a Camp Fire leader, or to attend their various events. Do your best to find a job that will permit some freedom to do those things.

4. Don't try to be supermom! Keep meals simple, laundry done, and the house neat-look-

ing. The deep cleaning can wait till they're off to college.

5. To be certain you don't feel guilty about the children having to help too much, pay them a little bit for really big jobs. I believe a family is a team in which everyone contributes to the whole. But a bit of extra money can be used to teach money management to kids.

6. Be sure to take care of yourself in such areas as exercising, getting adequate sleep, teaching family members to help with housework, and by scheduling time for reading, prayer, and doing your favorite things. While it is often so tempting to overwork, your attention to these matters is vital.

I'm confident the Bible is correct when it tells us in Phil. 4:19, "And my God will supply every need of yours according to his riches in glory in Christ Jesus." Count on it; draw on it; the account is infinite!

DON'T BE GULLIBLE

"Mom, I hate you! I wish you were dead!" said little Jeannette. Only seven years old, she had learned the lesson of manipulation early! Her mother, long-suffering as she was, tried to explain once more why Jeannette could not eat cookies just before dinner. But when this hostility poured out of her mouth, Mom—who did not want to be hated *or* dead—gave in. "Well, OK. Just one." Once more Jeannette had won. With a big smile she forgot the anger and happily ate the cookie. True to Mom's prediction, she was unable to eat a healthy dinner.

Like Jeannette, children learn early which button to push to get their way. Through anger and bullying, tears and drama, or wiles and charm, they will test your motherly strength and wisdom. You must not give in because children sorely need secure boundaries in order to learn to make adjustments in life.

Where do children learn the fine art of manipulation? I really suspect some children are born with the knack. But many of them learn from their mothers. When a mom tries too often to distract a one-year-old from the light socket by offering a cookie, she may well be sowing the seeds of the child's later conning her. When she asks her two-year-old if the toddler would *like* to put away the toys and take the usual nap, Mom is trying to manipulate her child. When Mom excuses any child's rudeness because he or she is "tired," she is teaching the skill of making excuses—manipulating.

So, moms, be aware of how you train your tiny child. Be clear and definite with the needed restrictions. Stick with an issue, whatever it may be, until your baby of a year or so understands what is off-limits. Strive for 100 percent consistency. Later, he or she will be prepared for more difficult rules. When you set a limit for your child, do so thoughtfully because you will need to follow through unfailingly. This is how a child learns obedience. Having learned it with you will one day make it easier to submit to school and community authorities. Best of all, by teaching obedience and respect, your child is certainly going to find it easier, more natural, to submit to the authority of the Heavenly Father.

It's a struggle to stay honest with your child and to carefully avoid being gullible or easily tricked. Mothering is never easy, but the rewards last a lifetime.

DO COMMUNICATE

Healthy families have good communication skills. We've already discussed the importance of good listening and of not lecturing children. But there's more to it than that. Great communication must include the following ingredients:

1. *Focus on the issue at hand.* Perhaps you want 16-year-old Sylvia to do her English paper and clean her room. She, of course, would rather talk with her friends and go shopping. This conflict is old stuff, and you are getting

pretty fed up. How tempting it is to remind Syl that she *always* resists her duties and *never* keeps her room clean. Good communication does not bring up past issues or irrelevant topics. Stick with this problem, work out the answer, and then express appreciation.

2. *Use as few words as possible.* Making a point depends on wise thinking, distilled into only a few words. Mothers usually want their kids not only to obey them but also to like doing it. They talk too much in order to reach those two goals. I find children are not likely to want to give up their pursuits in order to please Mom. So don't waste your energy on the impossible. They only have to *do* it—not *like* it!

3. *Share your life with your children.* When there is a friendly atmosphere, briefly share an interesting event or idea of your day. Tell stories now and then about your childhood and your parents. Children deserve to know about their heritage. It helps them learn who they are. And you are the best informant. Being open and honest must, of course, be balanced with good judgment. You may not choose to reveal some of your darker secrets!

4. *Learn to read body language.* The way kids of-

ten talk can be quite different from their facial expressions. Given a choice, I always believe body language. A tight mouth and clenched fists depict anger—which always is a cover-up for pain. Boys hate to cry, but you will see moisture in their eyes. If you will ignore rude or hostile words and say, "I see you looking sad (or hurt)," you will very often help your child open up.

5. *Guide your child to find answers.* Good communication is a teaching opportunity. Ask questions, and lead your kids to think wisely.

6. *After the emotion subsides, discuss any rudeness during disagreements.* Hostility explodes and problems go untouched when you detour into scolding about bad words or anger. Once again, solve the problem, then work on other issues one at a time.

"Evil communications corrupt good manners," writes Paul in 1 Cor. 15:33 (KJV). Be sure to keep your communication positive.

DON'T BE A WORRIER

Mickey had prompted the 10th call from his teacher to his mom in two weeks. It seemed he was always getting into trouble and dragging Mom with him. On Monday they both sat with his fourth grade teacher and even the principal! As Mickey lifted his downcast gaze from the floor to Mom's face, here's what he saw—a deeply furrowed brow, eyes brimming with tears, a trembling chin. He knew Mom was terribly worried about him. And here's what he thought: "I must be about as bad as a guy can get. I can't be good enough, but I sure am mean enough."

Adults know how Mickey's mom felt. Most of us have worried about our kids—some of those fears based in reality, but some also imagined. In fact, we don't worry unless we deeply care about someone. But habitually ornery behavior by a child can make worry become a mom's paramount emotion regarding him. And, like Mickey, such worry communicates negative ideas about himself. Children, like adults, act and look as they think and feel. So help your child feel good about himself.

Here's how you can help a mischievous child learn to feel great and act better:

1. Solve the problem of the misbehaviors. Be extremely clear about the rules and expectations. Be equally definite about the consequences if those rules are broken. Follow through every time.

2. Look as hard for your child's good qualities as you have done for the wrongdoing. Every time you catch him or her doing any-

thing good, remark positively about it. Now don't get gushy; just don't miss it!

3. Develop your own plans for stopping the worry. My plan is this:

    a. Define exactly what the problem is. If you don't know, keep asking others until you do.

    b. With help, if needed, formulate a solution to the problem and a plan for working it out.

    c. Be definite and energetic about working on it. Set time deadlines; and if progress is too slow, find out how to improve the way you're working.

    d. Don't hesitate to seek help: from a school counselor, a relative or friend, or a professional therapist if necessary. Even the high cost of such help is worth your sacrifice if it saves your child.

    e. Talk with God. He has made Christ to be our Wisdom (1 Cor. 1:30). Take advantage of that!

As you conquer your habit of worrying about your child, you will free him or her to become all God desires.

DON'T BE MOODY

Children are born with a tendency to either a happy or a blue mood. If you came into the world as one of the latter, it may not take much to tip your emotional balance to the dark side, even as an adult. Neglect by your husband or a friend, stubborn resistance from your child, a failed attempt at decorating or cooking—any of these can result in a down mood.

Certainly you are entitled to your own feelings. They are always understandable and related to life experiences. Trouble is your children invariably believe that your mood was created by them so they feel guilty and scared. They need a mom who emanates peace, love, and joy.

So what's a mom to do? How can she be honest and still put on the emotional veneer her family needs? Not an easy assignment!

When my children were attending elementary school, I knew they needed a good breakfast and a pleasant mother. But I was *not* a morning person. I found myself short-tempered, and silently I poured a little cold cereal into a bowl and dumped in the milk. Often we parted with grouchiness or tears!

But I didn't like this climate. And my morning mood was causing it. With heroic effort, I forced myself to get up earlier (never early!) and went around to each child's bed and kissed or tousled them awake. I cut a grapefruit and put a red cherry in the center, fixed a varying menu of the kids' favorite foods, prayed with them, and loved them off to school. I found that my mood changed as my behavior improved. So after all, I was honest.

Whatever your mood, or its cause, you, too, can change it. Consider these steps:

1. Name how you feel—sad, hurt, worried, or angry—whatever it is.
2. Concentrate until you figure out just why you feel that way.
3. With a prayer for guidance decide what you can do to correct the problem.
4. Then do that!

Be sure to explain to your children that you are feeling somewhat down, that you are working on it and will be OK. If you need their help, say so. But be specific, and avoid letting them feel responsible for either your mood or its correction. You and they can enjoy a life free of crippling moodiness!

DO ENJOY YOUR CHILD

As I'm writing, I'm looking at a little school picture of myself at the age of eight. My Dutch girl haircut frames my round face with wide-set hazel eyes and straight lips. It's a pleasant, even intelligent face, but without a smile. I found myself thinking somewhat sadly, "I wish my mom had known what a good child I was, how hard I tried to please her, what a sense of humor I hid behind that sober face!"

Because of her legalistic, rigid beliefs and her habit of worrying, my mother hardly enjoyed me. If she did, I never knew it! Both of us missed so much.

When I became a mother, I, too, took my job very seriously. Granted, I played with my children, and they brought me a wealth of pleasure and pride. But I stumbled into experiencing joy with them.

It happened on a lovely family vacation. On a warm afternoon my husband and I were resting in our hotel room when I became aware of peals of laughter from the children's room next door. A bit tentatively, I knocked on their door, and they graciously invited me in. They were telling funny stories about each other and various relatives. Perhaps it was their mood, but I found myself joining my laughter with theirs. It was an unforgettable experience.

That afternoon was a turning point in one aspect of my mothering. I knew that my children could balance the responsibility I knew with a hilarious joy I've never lost. To this day, I can ask one or the other of my three child friends, and they will tell some story that promises healthy laughter.

Sometimes, joy comes out of unexpected sources. Always it is a fruit of God's Holy Spirit. Look for it!

DON'T SPOIL YOUR CHILDREN

There are many ideas about what spoils children. Holding an infant too much, showing sympathy when a child is in some sort of pain, comforting a little one when he or she is scared at night—all of these have been labeled as spoiling children. None of them really is.

But it *is* possible to spoil a child—to change one from a joy to an annoyance, to transform one of yours from a pleasure to an irritation. Mother, you can prevent such a tragedy. Here's how:

1. Don't give in when you make a rule. Be very cautious about making rules, and carefully explain their reason for being. But once made, stick to them like glue. Every child is secure and becomes productive only when he or she learns to follow the rules of home, or the laws of the community and of God.

2. Don't give your child too many *things*. Give all the love, both tough and tender, that's in your heart. But children who get everything they think they want become tyrants. They demand more and more but value things

less and less. Children need to yearn deeply for special things. They value them most when they have to wait for them awhile, work to earn part of their cost, and are required to take care of them. If we too readily replace items that are broken or lost through carelessness, we teach children to be irresponsible and ungrateful.

3. Don't expect too little. As I've said before, children who have no duties, whose mothers do too much for them, have little of which to be proud. They grow up irresponsible and expect the world to pamper them as Mom did. Know your child's abilities well enough so you can require him or her to measure up to them. Constantly be aware of seeking the balance between expecting the impossible and requiring only minimal effort. Don't spoil your child's eventual success by allowing him or her to get by with only halfhearted efforts.

Spoiled children usually grow up to be rotten adults. And someday you will need the support of your adult children. Train them well, then, while you can!

DO BE A PLACE FOR RETURNING

Years after I was married and had my own home and three children, regularly I made the journey to my childhood home. Today's family characteristically moves many times. From before my birth, my family never moved. Every time we drove up to the old white house, Mother greeted us from the kitchen window. Dad and the collie dog would be walking from the barn to help us carry in our bags. After a wonderful visit full of love and nurturing, they would wave good-bye from the back stoop as we left.

I trust I told them enough how secure their stability made me feel. They have been in heaven for several decades, but their legacy of strength still enriches my life.

The old house is gone, replaced by a fine brick bungalow. The barn where I flew from the highest rafters to the soft bed of new-mown hay exists only in my memories. But nearby, the small, white country church remains unchanged. Whenever I can, I make a pilgrimage to the lovingly tended cemetery beside it. There I sit and remember—my mother's prayers, my father's playfulness, the hard work and energetic games we played. From these enormously rich memories, I find a few tears. But mostly, I find gentle smiles, remembered lessons about all aspects of life, and a deep sense of strength. Home was for me, and still is, a haven in an often heartless world.

By practicing these few dos and don'ts, I pray that you, mothers, by who you are, will be like that home and my mother were to me—a place for returning, for refilling by God's grace my spiritual resources.